US edition 2016; 2024
Hardcover edition 2019; 2024

ISBN-13: 978-0-578-57045-7

Illustrations by Rob Peters in pen, ink, and 6B pencil on Bristol paper and digitally painted in Photoshop.

All matters regarding weight management and health require medical supervision. The author is not engaged in rendering professional advice or services to children and their families or caregivers. The ideas, procedures, and suggestions contained in this book are not intended as substitutes for consulting with your medical-care provider. All matters regarding schools and their policies on bullying should be directed to appropriate school personnel. The author shall not be liable or responsible for any loss or damage allegedly arising from information or suggestions in this book. The author does not assume any responsibility for errors or for changes that occur after publication. The author does not have any control over and does not assume any responsibility for author or third-party websites or their content.

For Children
Who Have Experienced
Weight-Based Name-Calling

—RRB

Foreword

Please Don't Call Me Chubby Roni! is a story about the harm of name-calling in the school setting for a young girl. The action taken by the main character, Roni, and her teacher raise awareness about weight-based bullying in the classroom. The book serves to open communication with children, parents, and teachers about negative body-size talk and the impact it can have on children. Questions for discussion are included for children, teachers, and parents.

The Roni Children's Book Series (www.ronichildrenseries.com) is an educational and engaging teaching tool for school-age children and their families. The series supports the establishment of nonthreatening and wholesome environments to help children grow, learn, and accomplish their dreams.

Other books in the series are:
Roni Takes Action;
Roni Goes to Camp; and,
Roni Discovers Mindfulness: Introducing Kids to Eating and Living in a Mindful Way

Thanks to Adrienne Forman, MS, RDN, a children's weight-management specialist for suggesting the book's title and providing valuable comments.

I opened my closet and looked inside. School pictures were scheduled for the next day.

"I want to look really good," I whispered to myself.

Then I saw it—my favorite dress!

I took it out of the closet and arranged it on the chair with my socks and shoes for school the next morning.

"Mom," I said while I ate my breakfast, "I want to look awesome for my school picture today. Will you help me with my hair?"

Most of the time, my hair was a mess in the morning. I was always in a rush to get to school on time. But this day was special.

At school, my class went to the auditorium for individual student pictures.

When it was my turn, I sat on a stool in front of a blue-and-white school banner.

To get my attention, the photographer shouted, "Ravioli!"

I sat perfectly still with a big grin on my face.

One by one, all the students had their pictures taken.

As I watched, I said to Jackie, "Some kids are short, and some are tall. We come in all shapes and sizes, don't we?"

"Just like a box of animal crackers," Jackie replied.

We both giggled.

Next, the class stood in line for the group picture. I was one of the tallest in our class, which made me feel awkward.

Sarah, another tall girl, said, "Roni, don't feel bad. Kids grow and develop at different rates."

"How do you know?"

"My mom's a doctor," Sarah replied.

"Oh," I said. "I guess that's why we all come in different shapes and sizes."

The photographer started shuffling us around on the stage. He placed me in the middle of the group for the class picture.

"I don't like being in the middle," I told Max, a boy standing next to me.

"One day I'll be taller than you, Roni," Max predicted.

That made us both laugh.

A few weeks later, I found a large envelope with the class photo on my desk.

I started to open it.

Then Sam, the boy at the desk next to mine, yelled, "Hey, **Chubby Roni,** is that you in the middle of the class picture?"

Some of the kids laughed, and my face turned bright red.

I'd never been called **chubby** before, and it hurt!

After school, I ran straight home, opened the front door, threw my backpack on the floor, went up the stairs to my room, and slammed the door shut.

"Roni," Nana said, knocking on my door. "How was your day at school? Why did you run up to your room without saying hello?"

I didn't answer. She knocked again.

"Roni, are you all right?"

I opened the door and said, "Hi, Nana."

"You seem upset, Roni. What happened? How was your day at school?"

"Not good," I replied.

She looked concerned. "Let's go downstairs and talk about it."

13

Downstairs, Nana said, "Do you want to tell me what happened at school today?"

She went to pick up my backpack. I said quietly, "Nana, look inside."

She pulled out the class photo. "Oh, my! Roni, why is your picture scratched out?"

I took the photograph from her. "Sam, a boy in my class, made fun of my picture and called me **chubby.**"

Nana was speechless.

At the kitchen table, Nana said, "Roni, it hurts when a classmate is mean. You don't deserve to be spoken to that way by another student or by anyone."

She looked me straight in the face. "Roni, I understand how you feel. I'm sure you will know what to do."

Later that evening, I was doing homework when Dad came into my room.

"Roni, you're upset," he said. "Hurtful comments about appearance are unacceptable. Would you like me to speak with the boy, his parents, and your teacher?"

I just sat at my desk, feeling numb.

Then Mom joined us.

"Roni, often kids are picked on for looking different."

She lowered her voice and said caringly, "No matter what shape or size a person is, it's important to accept oneself and take steps to be healthy, like we do as a family."

Before leaving my room, she turned to me and said, "You are my pride and joy. Remember, we are always here to help."

17

I tossed and turned the whole night.

"What am I going to do?" I kept repeating to myself. "I can't let Sam get away with calling me **chubby**."

"Kids grow and develop at different rates, as my friend Sarah told me. I'm not going to feel bad about myself."

"I must be brave," I thought.

when I got to school the next day, I was scared. What if Sam said something else hurtful to me and embarrassed me in front of the class?

I took a deep breath and walked up to Sam. I said, "Please don't call me Chubby Roni!"

He looked surprised, as if he'd forgotten what he had said to me the day before.

I said again, "Please don't call me Chubby Roni!"

As I walked back to my desk, Rosa, my best friend, and a few other girls gathered around me. "Good for you, Roni!"

Ms. Chen, our teacher, had overheard what I'd said to Sam.

"Sit down, girls," she said. "Go back to your desks. Class is starting."

20

Ms. Chen stood in front of the class as usual, but this morning was different.

She spoke to us clearly and firmly. "Words are powerful. Name-calling is not tolerated in my class."

Then she went to the board and started listing words.

Chubby   Scrawny

Fat   Small

Heavy   Skinny

Husky   Slim

Plump   Thin

"Who can tell me why I wrote these words on the board?" she asked.

"The words are about body size," Max said.

"Go on," she said.

"The words in the first column are similar to one another, and so are the words in the second column. But the first- and second-column words are opposites."

Max added in a soft voice, "Calling someone fat or skinny is unkind."

Ms. Chen then asked, "Do these words describe how healthy we are?"

The whole class said, "NO."

Ms. Chen pointed to the board and said, "These words are hurtful. Let's remember to be kind to each other."

Chubby   Scrawny

Fat   Small

Heavy   Skinny

Husky   Slim

Plump   Thin

Ms. Chen asked us to arrange our desks in four groups.

Then, she said, "Your assignment today is to develop wellness recommendations in four categories. The categories are food, fitness, feelings, and friends. Each group will work on one category. After lunch, each group will share their recommendations with the class."

FITNESS

At lunch, Sam came over to me.

"Roni, I'm sorry for calling you **chubby.** At home, my dad calls my sister **chubby,** and I didn't think it was bad."

I said, "Sam, it's not OK for anyone to use words like that—not you, your dad, or anyone."

Back in class, the "food" group told us their list of healthy recommendations:

*   Eat fruits and vegetables often.

*   Eat a variety of foods at each meal.

*   Enjoy breakfast every morning.

*   Limit sugary drinks, cake, candy, chips, and cookies.

*   Drink plenty of water every day.

*   Choose reasonable portions, not supersized portions.

The "fitness" group shared their list next:

* Get some exercise every day, like bicycling, dancing, walking, or any physical activity you like to do.

* Limit time spent watching TV, using the computer, or playing video games.

* Get enough sleep.

* Practice safety, like wearing a bike helmet.

* Have fun being active.

Then the "feelings" group talked about their recommendations:

* Feel good about yourself.

* Ask for help if someone makes you feel bad.

* Think positive thoughts.

* Smile often.

* Be your best self.

The "friends" group came last:

* Stay away from mean kids. Let them know it's not OK to be hurtful to others.

* Talk to a best friend or family member if you are worried about something.

* Seek out understanding adults at school, like a school counselor or favorite teacher.

* Be kind to others.

After school that day, I breathed a sigh of relief, knowing that Ms. Chen would not tolerate name-calling in class.

Nana was right. I had been able to figure out how to handle a bad situation with the support of my family, friends, and teacher.

I repeated to myself my motto: "Doing is freeing. Free to be the best that I can be."

Afterword

Children deserve the support of family members and other caring adults, especially teachers, to combat the harm that can result from weight-based name-calling and bullying, whether at school, at home, in the neighborhood, or online.

Recognizing weight-based bullying is an important way to prevent children from feeling alone and powerless. Effective strategies in school and at home are necessary to protect children who are ostracized and stigmatized because of body size and appearance.

This book was written to help teachers, parents, and caregivers navigate this sensitive subject with children.

All children should strive to be healthy, have a positive body image, and feel good at any size. There's no better gift we can give a child.

Questions for Discussion

For children, to recognize weight-based name-calling:

Have you ever been called hurtful names or teased because of your body weight, size, or appearance?

How did it make you feel?

Who was responsible for hurting you?

Has this person called you names before?

Did your friends or classmates stick up for you?

Have you told your parents, grandparents, teachers, or school counselors about these negative comments?

For all children, to raise awareness about weight-based name-calling:

Is it OK to call someone fat, fatso, fatty, twiggy, scrawny, toothpick, or similar negative body image words?

How would you feel if someone made a hurtful comment about your appearance?

Would you stand up and support a kid who is being teased about his or her appearance?

Do you think male and female models in fashion magazines represent how all of us should look?

Do professional sports players all look alike? Who do you admire?

Are you aware that we all come in many shapes and sizes and that we come from different families, cultural backgrounds, and traditions?

How can we be sensitive to all children and promote kindness, no matter what shape or size others may be?

For teachers, to prevent weight-based name-calling at school:

Are you alert for weight-based name-calling in the classroom, in the lunchroom, in the school hallway, and on the playground?

Have you shared your concerns with students and parents?

Is there a support system in place at school to help children who have been victimized because of body weight?

What classroom strategies can be implemented to embrace a no-tolerance policy for weight-based name-calling?

For parents, to increase awareness about the consequences of weight-based bullying in school or online:

Have you noticed uncommon signs or behavior in your child that may signal a problem at school, online, or elsewhere?

Ask your child the following questions: Have you been made fun of, called names, or teased at school or on social media? Is your classroom teacher supportive of you? What about other teachers? Can we work together to remove social media accounts that are harmful, as well as to delete unwanted individuals on those sites?

Ask yourself and your child what you can do to help. If necessary, request a referral to a mental-health professional skilled in this field from the school counselor or your child's medical provider.

Recommended Online Resources

American School Health Association

www.ashaweb.org

CDC Centers For Disease Control and Prevention

www.cdc.gov

Obesity Action Coalition

www.obesityaction.org

The BULLY Project

www.thebullyproject.com

United States (U.S.) Department of Health and Human Services

www.stopbullying.gov

University of Connecticut Rudd Center for Food Policy and Obesity

www.uconnruddcenter.org/weight-bias-stigma

WebMD

www.webmd.com/parenting/raising-fit-kids/
weight/talk-obesity-bullying

About the Author

As an advanced-level nutrition practitioner, **Dr. Roni Roth Beshears** has worked at the local, state, and federal levels with food and nutrition programs and services. As a community volunteer and advocate, she has devoted time and energy to serving the needs of vulnerable women, children, and families. Dr. Roth Beshears is a registered dietitian nutritionist and certified health and wellness coach. She is a graduate of Syracuse University (BS, cum laude) and Columbia University, Teachers College (EdD).

For additional information, please visit the Roni Children's Book Series website. www.ronichildrenseries.com

www.ingramcontent.com/pod-product-compliance
Lightning Source LLC
Chambersburg PA
CBHW040257100426
42811CB00011B/1288